Andrew was born in wartime England, into the austerity of Birmingham and the joy of weekends at his grandparent's Staffordshire farm.

Aged eight, the family moved to South Africa and after university in Johannesburg, he spent 10 years at Cambridge, studying quantum physics and mathematics, and became interested in Zen Buddhism.

After a career as an academic at various British universities, he took early retirement and trained as an actor, performing in numerous productions on the fringe and on tour.

Having spent twenty years restoring an old farmhouse in Normandy, he now divides his life between the Highlands of Scotland, Wiltshire and South Africa.

He has recently set up a charity supporting ecological education and research in South Africa.

To my wife.

Andrew Rae

TRANSCENDENCE

AUSTIN MACAULEY PUBLISHERS
LONDON * CAMBRIDGE * NEW YORK * SHARJAH

Copyright © Andrew Rae 2024

The right of Andrew Rae to be identified as author of this work has been asserted by the author in accordance with sections 77 and 78 of the Copyright, Designs and Patents Act 1988.

All rights reserved. No part of this publication may be reproduced, stored in a retrieval system, or transmitted in any form or by any means, electronic, mechanical, photocopying, recording, or otherwise, without the prior permission of the publishers.

Any person who commits any unauthorised act in relation to this publication may be liable to criminal prosecution and civil claims for damages.

A CIP catalogue record for this title is available from the British Library.

ISBN 9781035868513 (Paperback)
ISBN 9781035868520 (ePub e-book)

www.austinmacauley.com

First Published 2024
Austin Macauley Publishers Ltd®
1 Canada Square
Canary Wharf
London
E14 5AA

I would like to express my gratitude to the Reverend Jennifer Totney who encouraged my writing and to my wife Patrica for her endless support and encouragement.

A number of the poems have appeared in Areopagus Magazine.

Art work copyright Leigh Voigt.

Table of Contents

Foreword — 11
Nature — 13
   The Chalk Stream — 15
   Winter Beeches — 16
   The Monastery of Leaves — 17
   The Snail — 18
   Buffelskloof — 19
   The Waterfall — 20
   The Strangler Fig and the Myrrh — 21
   The Snake Eagle — 22
   The Moor in Spring — 23
   The Flower — 24
   Wilderness — 25

Church Buildings — 27
   A Wiltshire Church — 29
   The Church Tower — 30
   Church Lane — 31
   The Lane that Flowed — 32
   The Saxon Church — 33
   Highland Graveyard — 34
   St Wulfstan's Crypt Worcester Cathedral — 35
   The Columns of San Miniato — 36
   Lucca, Il Duomo — 37
   Convento di San Marco — 38
   St Leonard — 39
   La Merveille — 40

Literal Translation of La Merveille	42
Meditations	**45**
Hope	47
Prayer	48
On Reciting Racine	49
The Holy Letter	50
Despair	51
Downcast Mind	52
Peace that passes all understanding	53
Grace	54
Church Seasons	**55**
Advent	57
Advent at St Mary's	58
Candlemass	59
Ash Wednesday	60
Waiting for Easter in the Highlands	61
Whitsun	62
Trinity Sunday	63
Lockdown	**65**
Grace II	67
Lent in Lockdown	68
Easter after Lockdown	69
Midsummer in Lockdown	70
Memories	71
Rage	72

Foreword

Many people feel a sense of transcendence in front of the wonders of nature, the beauties of music and art, the miracles of birth and the tragedy of death.

These poems chart my own journey, starting from such experiences and connecting with my early religious education by Anglican monks of the Community of the Resurrection.

Sadly, in early manhood, I lost my faith. Later, worn down by life's struggles, I came back to religion in the form of Zen Buddhism and now, in old age, have found a spiritual home in the ancient rituals of the Anglican Church.

Nature

The Chalk Stream

I watch the river flowing,
I feel the sun upon my face,
then I think of all the suffering,
and I bend my head in sorrow.

But the limpid, moving water,
the weed so graceful, waving,
the eternal chalk stream full of life,
make memories flow around me.

Old disasters lose their sorrow,
now in sun by limpid water,
happiness seems all around.

I lose myself in contemplation
at one with stones and water,
untroubled by the fear of dying
like an animal, a bird, a flower.

Then I feel the water flowing,
and the sun upon my brow,
then I see the ripples shimmering,
and feel the waving grass below the water.
All is quiet, and I believe in God again.

Marlborough, September 2022

Winter Beeches

The trees were graceful,
their grey and slender curves
sublimely rising,
lit by the cool morning light;

brighter now
than when the summer sun,
shaded by a thousand dancing leaves,
sang quietly overhead.

Their elegance and beauty,
their eternal quietness,
indifferent to our strife,
our joys, sorrows, triumphs and despairs,

older than us, seeming eternal,
lifting gently into the air,
quietly seeding, feeding, growing.

They humble us
in our quiet despair;

giving hope in our winter darkness,
courage to continue living,
despite the threats and gloom
around us.

Wiltshire, December 2021

The Monastery of Leaves

I hear the crowded voices
        of humanity in distress,
here in my golden shelter,

the sun low on dewy grass,
        filtered through the last few leaves.

I hear it dimly, at peace in my winter arbour,
as my own life draws to its close.

What can I do to *mend the world,*

but pray for peace
        in my green monastery of leaves,

golden with birdsong, green with the sun,
        rich with worms, bacteria, and leaves.

Wiltshire, November 2022

The Snail

A very small grey snail
was on my table,
its body frozen into jelly,

yet its shell's fine, grey coil,
perfect in its symmetry,
sang strongly in the gloom,

told of the life force
even in its death,

spoke so loudly in its innocence,
in its quiet death,

of God who lies
in all things.

Wiltshire, December 2020

Buffelskloof

Buffalo Gorge, Land of the Rising Sun; a wild and ancient place.

A place
where the presence of God
rises like mist
beneath your feet.

There, silence speaks louder than thunder,
and trees hang darker than grapes.
A wilderness
wild as swallows,
a darkness bright in the autumn sun,

where leaves lie
undisturbed for centuries.

A wilderness
where the bones of women and children,
once white in the sun,
are crumbled now to dust between the leaves,

where a ghost-like leopard,
all fiery-eyed,
flits between the airy branches,

and leaves my soul to wonder
at what lies behind
this sunlit world,
what lies beyond
this teeming life,

something too deep for thought,
open only to prayer.

Wiltshire, 2017

The Waterfall

After *O Fons Bandusiae* by Horace.

Whiter than lightening, your growling surges,
worthy of fine whisky your clear water,
drifting with petals, your black-rocked pool.

Tomorrow perhaps the leaping fawn,
        dancing from ledge to rocky cleft,
                caught by the eagle's claw,
will stain with blood
        your icy stream,
his budding horns will fall on rocks,
        lost to love and battle,
        lost to leaping, dancing peers.

Even in bright winter's drought, your humble trickle
waters scorpion and snake,
        bristling boar and great-horned stag,
                spotted cat and jostling baboon.

And I will spread the fame
        of your proud falling,
of your black rocks and gleaming, towering cliffs,
        where fern and frond
        and blue love flower
drink your airy dew.

Buffelskloof, 2018

The Strangler Fig and the Myrrh

Entwined in a doomed embrace,
the strangler fig and the myrrh
tell of mortality.

A butterfly, strong as a bird,
flies from the foaming top of the falls,
across the rippling pool,
high into the trees.

Above, a sky like a crocodile's back,
drifts blue and white.

Below the sky,
high between the trees, a spider sits,
its web invisible against the cloud,

and I pray for all this beauty,
pray it will not die.

Buffelskloof, 2018

The Snake Eagle

Dark eagle,
    yellow eye.
Never soars,
    he hunts from a dead branch.
Fearless he stares,
      his huge wings folded.
For so long he eyes me,
    that yellow, unblinking eye,
moves his great feet,
    clasps his yellow claws around the branch,
        strong enough, quick enough,
to tear the fearsome mamba from his hole.
To kill and eat,
    Black, dark, and vicious,
      timorous, croaking, most deadly snake of all.

He looks, I look,
    he has no need to hide,
    or fear.

A great wild boar, all tusks and rufous hair, walks by ... the day drifts on.

At last, he moves,
    his wide wings spread out,
    he glides down across the rocks.

He does not deign to soar,
    just leaves and glides to another perch.

The valley opens and empties again.

Moved by this moment of
    I and thou
with this fearless yellow eye,

I feel myself enhanced,
a little closer even to God
    who made this strange and terrible world.

Buffelskloof, 2018

The Moor in Spring

When the bog myrtle blooms,
and gossamer glows white in the pearly dark,
when primrose banks shine bright in the shade,
and the roe deer runs lightly into the scrub,

when towering birches, festooned with feathery lichens,
shine softly green in morning light,
and a dusty lace-wing fly hovers over the dormant heather,

then my soul breathes again,
opens to life, deaf now to regret,
open to hope.

Glenshee, May 2019

The Flower

So gentle in the sunlight,
so lonely now and holy.
So white and pure your petals,
so fragile, new, and lonely,
hope held golden in your cup.

I knelt beside you on the grass,
above the river flowing,
beneath the birch tree budding.

The sunlight held me
for a moment, safe.

But now the birds, so busy,
chatter, sing, and bustle,
while far away a farmer
breaks the sleeping silence.

I held you in my heart,
a moment in the grass,
all green and lovely round me
in the sun which cannot last.

The hill was dark and purpled,
the sky was blue as fire,
and all around was holy.

Glenshee, spring 2014

Wilderness

The high, bare mountains,
savage rocks, grey screes, and lonely, misshapen trees,
every crevice rich in life: leaves
feathery, hairy, spiny,
reaching for the light, arching, drooping.

Boulders breeding green-grey lichen,
creeping bushes, berries black, blue, and red,
a panorama of fruitfulness.

And all the hidden living creatures
that moss and bog and stones conceal,
the insects, beetles, moths, and midges,

where man's ugly footprint
hardly shows.
Where stags still roar

the wilderness,
the desert where Jesus went to pray,
waiting for God to speak.

Glenshee, August 2023

Church Buildings

A Wiltshire Church

A place
       where the peace of God
descends like a cloud
       too quiet for sound too near for speech,
too low to hear
       too far to see.

A place
       where quietness lies,
where peace and justice intermingle,
       where love and hope hold hands in silence,
where God speaks softly,

and we are comforted

where hearts are opened,
       sorrows quietened,

where the spirit of life
       meets the sadness of death.

Even in winter as rooks fly up
       and stubble lies awry,
church bells call
       and the peace of God
which passes all understanding
       beckons welcome

in the quiet of ancient stones
       and the ghosts of forgotten sorrows
             consoled
                   long ago
in prayer.

Wiltshire, February 2017

The Church Tower

The Church Tower stands beside the manor.
Its grey stones gleam with centuries of hope,
its four spires reach up quietly heavenwards;
here black-robed friars once processed at midnight,
to pray to the light that's always pure,
psalms rising heaven ward in the cold black night.

Their bones were found beneath the manor's kitchen,
lined up in rows,
then moved to a safer place.

And now I walk past, through mud and mire,
whistling a humble tune,
as people have for a thousand years,
touched for a moment by the sublime:
the history of faith and bells and psalms;
feeling my own humanity again,
in this grey world of ours.

Wiltshire, Boxing Day 2020

Church Lane

Along the lane, buttresses hold gaily crumbling stone,
as soaring, bare-branched trees rise, white in the morning light,
and mist obscures the mossy walls,
gently curving down the lane,
so quiet, so still, so inexorably slow,
the crumbling wall.

Centuries passed
in my teaming brain's anxious questioning:
images of past glories, long-gone heroes,
black-clad monks, sorrows, plague, and death.

So, in a winter's stroll,
centuries of sorrow, peace, and joy
fly past me like a dream,

telling me to quietly sit and pray.

Wiltshire, January 2020

The Lane that Flowed

It seemed a flowing river,
full of souls departed now,
of people, friends, horses
who came this way.

It seemed to flow into the heart.

Whispering faces,
sad, old, shouting, crying,
back from battles long ago;

wailing pipes and haunting cuckoo,
singing of life that endures,
despite the dark and storms,
fears and threatening future.

Wiltshire, May 2022

The Saxon Church

The church is so old,
more than a thousand years,
so quiet and rustic,
its pulpit so near,
the panelling, the ancient curving beams,
the walls so close you can touch them,
a home, comforting,
no towering glory or gothic gloom.

One feels no need to scrub one's hands,
to smarten up, so many farmer's hands,
men of the soil, of beasts and butterflies,
have worshipped here,
prayed for rain, mourned their dead
within its panelled walls,

a holy place,
rustic and enchanted.

Alton Barnes, August 2022

Highland Graveyard

No-one cares now.
People pass,
while stones stay, bird song lingers, endlessly repeated,
but humans go,

leave only a dark stone nestled in grass,
its letters mossed and lichened, undecipherable.
while all the dark creatures of the soil
run, crawl, and creep, enjoy the peaty quiet.

Who left that stone?
Some brawny farmer, strong from days long in the heather,
days and nights of bitter weather,
trudging, struggling, with a beast across his back?

Now quiet and lonely is the glen,
its pastures raided by great herds of deer.
Its dykes lie crumbling where once the giant drank deep
and threw a golden cup to live for ever in the dark and peaty pool.

Now all that strong life, fierce in limb,
in muscled thigh and solid arm,
those centuries of fight and laughter and struggle against the dark,
all gone now, all quiet.

The spring bee sips gently from a flower,
the wee bird falls from its nest,
deer bark, hares peer and cuckoos call,

leave only the list of men who died in battle,
so many, and now so few,
so quiet rests the glen.

Glenshee, 2015

St Wulfstan's Crypt
Worcester Cathedral

A sepulchre once, Byzantine in its purity of marble, line, and curve,
telling of a faith, a style, simple in its holiness,
peaceful in its whiteness.

Remembered now among green fields,
the crypt glows in memory,
its white arches encircling his tomb for 900 years.

St Wulfstan left them for us,
a legacy to heal the soul, to free the troubled mind.
So white, so delicate,
intricately arching around the altar,

a sepulchre no more.

Wiltshire, 2017

The Columns of San Miniato

A holy place,
wide with columns,
huge, antique stone;

in the crypt, the holy bones,
worshipped by the faithful
for two thousand years.

Above, tower polished stone,
gleaming marble and fading frescoes,

while in the dark below,
a hundred columns rescued from the fall of Rome

whisper quietly
his holy name.

Florence, September 2022

Lucca, Il Duomo

A Head of Christ in dark black wood,
old by a thousand years,
sublime and peaceful on the cross.

A woven basket of stone, a towering column,
marbles, pink and green, columns, towers,

a white miracle, the Duomo stands,
one among so many churches.

And by the door,
Saint Martin, so young,
so handsome, so brave on his shy horse.
A miracle in stone,
a wonder, all so fresh and real, so solemnly here,
a gallant young man divides his clothes,
gets out his sword,
to clothe the beggar in his finery.

Lucca, September 2022

Convento di San Marco

The Monk's Cells

In each cell,
      a masterwork,
for each monk,
      a masterpiece,
in delicate pastels,
      devotional,
an image for prayer,
      and fasting,

for some, the suffering,
for others, quiet joy,
adoration, and worship.

The Prior's Rooms

Savonarola
His black cloak, his hooded nose, his sombre eyes,
his cloak preserved,
      spread out for five hundred years;
his cruel death adorns his walls,
the smoke arises from his pyre.

A virgin and child
by his disciple, Fra Bartolomeo,
who loved him,
still hangs above his desk.

Florence, September 2022

St Leonard

He stands still, glorious in his corner,
elected bishop a millennium and more ago,
his hair, still young and blonde,
the colour still showing on his cloak;

pillars proudly surround his honest face.
A Jewish candelabrum stands devotional in a nook,
while on the paving, behind the mossy altar,
a butterfly shed its wings long ago last summer.

Now, under the green vaulting,
the ancient stones, the oak door,
and the dark twilight of the dome,

make my spirit breathe again,
as the weight of all my ancient sadnesses
flies up like smoke

to leave me whole again.

Avranches, 2017

La Merveille
(Le Mont Saint Michel)

Depuis l'îlot, comme d'une étoile les rayons de lumière,
étendent, en toutes directions,

les traces des pèlerinages,
visibles dans les noms des villages:

les Montjoies -
pour la première vue de la merveille, le Mont Saint Michel,

fondé suivant un rêve
par le bienheureux Aubert il y a mille ans et demi.

    La merveille, au péril des mers,
    une cathédrale perchée au sommet du rocher,
    entourée par monastère, cloitre et cloches,

    hantée par bernache et barge,
    survolée d'immense trainées d'oiseaux marins,

    entourée par sables mouvants, pièges des pêcheurs,
    par courants, marées et mascarets sauvages.

Les Chambres, *Le Repas*
parlent du commerce de pélerinage dans les jours d'antan.

Et encore ils viennent pour le Pardon,
le grand pèlerinage de juillet,

    quand pecheurs font la traversée sous l'égide de l'évêque,
après une messe à la grande église de Genêts,
    au péril des sables et courants,
    espérant peut-être une mort bienheureuse sous les flôts de la baie,

regardant le mont comme un mirage de ciel,
    entendant les anges dans les soufflées de la mer,
    laissant la côte, abri des salières et moutons du pré-salé,

marchant sur les traces des pièges à poisson
    âgés de trois mille ans

Et a l'ouest, sur la forêt submergée,
    s'ouvre l'océan,
    L'Atlantique

    source des orages, averses et ouragans,

    les Iles Chaussey, îlots de granite, abri des homards,

    et Granville, forteresse des Anglais,
    espérant saccager le mont et tous ses trésors,
    ses incroyables livres datant de l'époque romaine,
    ou décorés par les moines du passé en or et lapis lazulite.

Toujours brave,
abri des moines,
sanctuaire de la sainteté même,
protégé des saccageurs, les Goths, les Anglais
par la bénissante mer et les sables mouvants
même la révolution ne pouvait pas,
bien que transformé en prison,
le détruire.

Il reste encore
une merveille pour nos temps,
un refuge pour pénitent et touriste
ignorant l'histoire, l'église,

les orgueilleux qui ne connaissent que la chair,
arrivant par millions chaque été
pour respirer la paix, la douleur guérie,
la sainteté créée par les pélerins du monde entier,
en mille ans et demi.

Le Mont, la Merveille, au péril des mers.

Wiltshire, février 2022

Literal Translation of La Merveille

The Wonder

From the islet,
as from a star the rays of light,
extend in all directions,
the traces of pilgrimages,
visible in the names of the villages:

those called the 'Mount of Joy'
marking the first sight of the wonder,
the Mont St Michel,
founded after a dream by the blessed Aubain
a thousand and a half years ago;
the Wonder, 'in peril of the seas,'
a Cathedral perched on the summit of the rock,
surrounded by monastery, cloister, and bell,
haunted by goose and godwit,
overflown by immense trains of sea birds,
surrounded by quicksands, traps for shellfish gatherers,
by savage currents, tides, and bores;

those called 'The Rooms,' 'The Repast'
mark the last night before the dangerous crossing.

And still they come for:
'The Pardon,' the great pilgrimage each July,
when sinners walk the crossing of the bay under the aegis of the Bishop,
after a mass at the great church of Genéts,
at the mercy of sands and currents,
hoping perhaps for a blessed death under the waves of the bay,
seeing the Mont as a mirage of Heaven,
hearing angels in the breathing of the sea,
leaving the coast, protector of salt gatherers and salt marsh sheep,
marching over the traces of fish traps
laid three thousand years ago;

and to the West, past the drowned forest,
opens out the ocean,
the Atlantic:
source of storms, squalls, and hurricanes,
the Chaussey isles, granite homes for lobsters,
past Granville, fortress built by the English,
hoping to sack the Mont and all its treasures;
its incredible books, some Roman,
others decorated by ancient monks in gold and lapis lazuli.

Always brave,
shelter for monks,
a sanctuary for sanctity itself,
protected from Goths and English robbers
by the blessing sea and quicksands;
even the revolution failed,
despite transformation into a prison
to destroy it.
It remains still
a wonder for our times,
a refuge for penitent and tourist
knowing nothing of the history, of the church,
the proud who know of nothing but the flesh,
arriving in millions every summer
to breathe in the peace, the suffering cured,
the sanctity created by pilgrims from across the world
over a thousand and a half years.
The 'Mont', the 'Wonder', in peril from the seas.

Meditations

Hope

Hope is shy, hides quietly,
lost in shady cathedral corners.

Hope needs our trust,
despite our fear, alone in our thoughts,

for nature shouts and loudly calls:
"Yes, He is here!"
in every wilted flower or blade of grass,
on mountain peak or desert sand,

in laws of nature,
palaces of reason,
cancerous tumour
and cruel fire,

in torture cell
and empty void.

But hard it is to understand
His plan.

Wiltshire, February 2018

Prayer

I woke disturbed by angry thoughts,
resentment and disappointment,
but then I prayed my morning prayers,

recited the familiar words,
struggled to mean them:

a pure heart and a humble mind,
salvation and liberty,

and all at once, was filled
by a cloud of holy calm and peace.

Wiltshire, June 2023

On Reciting Racine

When I lie awake at night, I recite Racine's "Hymnes traduites du Breviaire Romain."

The architecture of his lines,
        the spaces, curves, volumes of sanctity,

his monkish life,
        his midnight orisons,
come alive
and comfort me.

His midnight sombre, his vigilant birds of sunrise,
his ardent prayer, weeping and groaning,
reaching the heavens

and Jesus close at hand.

Wiltshire, February 2020

The Holy Letter

Written by St Francis to Brother Leo c. 1227

The Holy letter,
just a scrap of paper,
his writing so clear

"*I write to you like a mother,*
the answer, so simple:
just follow Him,
follow the way.

Ask for help if you need it."

So quiet, so simple,
just love.

Wiltshire, May 2023

Despair

Ô miséricorde divine à la rencontre de mon désespoir*
(Psalm 6 vs 10 tr Paul Claudel)

Do we choose to fight against despair,
or flee into the mind of God?
Do we battle or believe?

In old age, I cannot fight.
I struggle to believe,
envy those gone on before,
long for rest.

*O the pity of God for me in my despair

Wiltshire, September 2021

Downcast Mind

I struggle with my downcast mind,
searching solace,
in ancient prayers and fervent gospels,
among tombs and airy angel roofs.

In graceful birds, immortal music,
in savage winds, lowering skies, and foetid sewers.

In kindness, charity, and calm.

In poems of troubled loves and ancient joys.

In daring harmonies and counterpoint.

In friends long dead.

In fields of cows,
in grass,
in nature's savage embrace.

In soil beneath my fingernails,
forgotten plants now flourishing.

In fruit trees budding,
promising autumn riches.

In memories of childhood,

the tenderness of friends,
the joys of science,
the promise of understanding.

and still my head hangs weary,
despair hovers,
and death laughs behind my shoulder blade.

sorrow must be born.
Sarvam Dukham*

* "Everything is bitter" The Buddha

Wiltshire, June 2019

Peace that passes all understanding

I walked down by the river,
long with hooting owls.

I floated on the tide,
pooled with gold and fragile shadows,

in this the evening of my life,
at peace with the world and God and all things.

Wiltshire, December 2022

Grace

Trees stand tall, red and gold,
branches dance a ghostly ballet.

Leaves lie on rich, dark earth,
ready for winter's rain and cold,
for living, hungry soil to take them, grasp them,
feed on them,
promising rebirth in the joy of spring.

So we must pray to God for grace to turn our dreams,
our selfish greed, our restless desires,
into hope and love,

to feed a new world,
to grow a springtime,
out of all our sadness
and despair.

Wiltshire, November 2021

Church Seasons

Advent

Yew berries,
drops of blood among the leaves,
remind us of His coming, to live and die among us.

Now is the season when we wait,
at year's end for a new beginning,
among the autumn riches,
the golden leaves, the ripened fruit.

As winter comes, we plough the purple soil and sow,
before the quiet days of winter's rest for seed and plant,
looking forward to His birth,
bringing grace and courage,
hope, forgiveness, and love
to teaming, suffering, labouring men and women
all across the world.

Let us find joy, despite the suffering,
look beyond the grief,
to find God's presence everywhere.

Let us remember his mercy,
see the joy of life reborn in every leaf and flower,
a mystery and a magic
that brings hope.

Hope is a duty,
born of prayer,
reborn in love,

and in worship.

Wiltshire, November 2021

Advent at St Mary's

The buds are swelling in the hedges,
dull red, green, and purple;
the mist drifts across the field,
greening now with summer's promise.

The swans are standing on the ice,
guarding their future nesting place,
as we sit waiting quietly for a sacred baby,
born in straw and candlelight.

A strong young voice sings of snow,
of winter's glory long ago,
and we are heartened, warmed.

A tear lurks in our eyes,
at magic, pain, and sacrifice,
at wonder, joy,
a glimpse of heaven,
to chase away the strife and cold,
the raucous voices,
and frightening gales.

Alton Barnes, December 2022

Candlemass

When hope fades and despair rules,
when everywhere are lies and fantasies,
when unjust rulers are full of hope,

while we, the would-be just, the would-be good and helpers to mankind,
see hunger, greed,
and power-crazed maniacs finding followers,

see brutal bigots and angry young men,
what hope is there for those in teaming, foetid slums?

But we are told to light a candle,
and pray for renewal.

Wiltshire, February 2021

Ash Wednesday

For you are dust,
And to dust you will return.
Genesis 3:19

Let us cover our bodies with haircloth and ashes,
and remember our sins,

as the cold days before spring
and emptying shelves
cool our bodies and minds.

Let us suffer our sins
in the sadness of shame,
as the cold wind of winter
calms body and brain.

As the sun starts to climb,
showing promise of spring
and purging of pain,
we may be whole again,
whole with His aid.

Alone, we are lost to sin and to death,
lost with dust in the fertile earth,

but with help, we may climb,
as the sun lightens the sky,

out of the pit
of sadness and shame.

Wiltshire, March 2018

Waiting for Easter in the Highlands

The river lay full and white,
under leafless trees and a pale sky.
A lamb's skull, white in the moss,
an ancient stump lay splintered.

The evening light was golden on the hill,
on lifeless heather and creeping willows,
clouds speckled an arctic sky,
and a bubbling curlew called, lazy, in the dusk.

All is peaceful here tonight,
while far away the guns are roaring,
people dying,
and children lie huddled in the cold.

Why is all the world so sad
this Maundy Thursday, waiting for Easter?

Will there be a new dawn,
after this agony?

Glenshee, April 2023

Whitsun

They sat in an upstairs room,
        disciples and followers,
mourning the loss of their resurrected Lord,
when a noise like a mighty wind
        filled their anguished ears.
Their hearts beat loud together,
        flames filled the air,
              they moaned, then cried with sudden joy.

The spirit of the church was born.

Together they cried and wept,
and knew their faith would last.

And rushing out,
        alight with joy,
they clasped and hugged
        all around,

who, astonished, first thought them drunk

then understood.

Wiltshire, May 2017

Trinity Sunday

The Creator,
we call God,
made reason, time and space.

Unknowable,
just, benign, powerful,
beyond knowledge or understanding.

His Son,
put into words
      the holiness of life.

His Spirit,
breathed upon us,
opened our eyes
to truth
and
love.

Wiltshire, May 2017

Lockdown

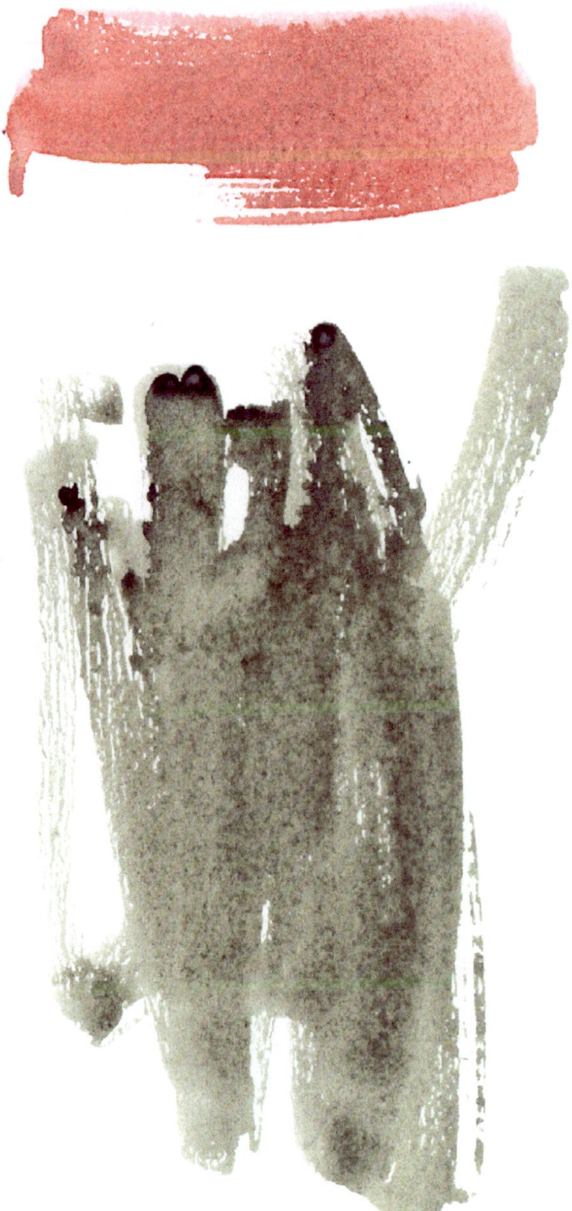

Grace II

I sit sadly,
in this drear and saddest year.
Friends and colleagues die,

and yet the bird song
brightly comes before the break of dawn,
even in the dark and rain,
in first light before the sun,
healing, warming, promising summer,

despite the winter's dark and cold;
when hope itself hides, death threatens,
and Grace is hard to find.

But Grace is all we have to hope for
in the gloom and threats around us,

to pray that Grace will find us,
the Grace of God
that passes all understanding.

Wiltshire, January 2021

Lent in Lockdown

Lent is time to feel the sadness in your bones,
as new growth brings memories of past,
and fear of future, loss and pain
in this time of plague and death.
Many will not see this year in bloom,
eat its harvest, or watch it grow.

More than ever, we need the help,
the hope, the grace, the love
of our Lord, the loving Master.
Courage to hope, to dig, to sow,
to love again, to plan the future,

to save the world from evil plunder,
from sadness and despair,
thoughtless greed and wish for death.

Wiltshire, March 2021

Easter after Lockdown

In this year of sorrows,
a light has come to free us,
giving strength again,
with memories slowly waking,
mental muscles stiffly creaking,
with hope of life and laughter,
remembered joys returning.
Fellowship in the evening,
life reborn in friendship,
sadness treasured quietly,
of love reborn within us,
of God all round about us,
forgiving us our sins.

Wiltshire, May 2021

Midsummer in Lockdown

In my green glade there is no summer.
In my dark heart there is no light.
In all the world my crazy sadness
looks for calm and solace,
in the owl-filled gloom of night.

The bright of midday is too much,
only the quiet buzzing of a fly
quietens my disquiet,
calms the teaming voices,

reminds me of the peace of God,
which passes all understanding.

Wiltshire, June 2021

Memories

Within the easy dark of memories,
along time's endless corridor,

I feel the soil still in my veins,
the rising sap, the falling leaves,
the easy triumphs, the quiet despair.

Now summer heat brings memories of joy,
of warmth, of love,
of swimming in the dark,
wild stream of my childhood,
alive with youth,

of loves won and lost,
battles fought and troubles,
dark troubles following.

Pride, complacency, easy laughter,
and guilt-ridden aftermath.

Then they told me about the Grace of God,
le salut et la liberté*

and now I dream my days away,
watching midges in the sun,
listening to the birds and farmers in the distance,

wrapped in a cocoon of love.

* salvation and freedom

Wiltshire, June 2021

Rage

When all the world seems full of fear,
and hate is blossoming in many a heart,
drowned in grief we cannot feel
for all the loved ones lost, we
can only rage
against the dying of the light.

Inshallah… it is the will of God
we are supposed to say,
but do we feel it in our hearts,
or do we cry:

Why have you forsaken me?

Our sins stand up accusingly.
They claim the blame.

There was one who came to save…
but can we believe it in our bones,
feel it, born as we are to die,
can we reach beyond our lockdown souls,
shut out from hope and love and life?

Somehow we must be strong,
however deep we lie,
lost in phantom-filled depths,
deep in a sea of sorrows,
far from all remembered joy.
Reach out we must, stretch out our locked down arms,
grow through the soil, the green of spring,
feel *ubuntu,* love for all humanity in its grief,

grow again in hope and life and love.

Wiltshire, May 2021